HANDS-ON PATTERNS AND PROPS

By Bonnie Bernstein
Illustrated by Corbin Hillam

Publisher: Roberta Suid
Contributing Editors: Elizabeth Russell,
Lillian Lieberman
Cover Design: David Hale
Design and Production: Mary Francis

ISBN 0-912107-21-9

Printed in the United States of America

9 8 7 6 5 4 3 2 1

CONTENTS

INTRODUCTION

This book is a kit for constructing learning materials that children can't wait to get their hands on — interactive bulletin boards, three-dimensional displays, flannel board games, mechanical toys, play mats, props. The attractive constructions serve two purposes: They add brightness to the classroom, and they offer manipulative experiences to reinforce cognitive learning. All are easy and inexpensive for teachers to put together, but sturdy enough to withstand lots of play.

Every idea has complete directions, illustrations, patterns or materials to be duplicated, and suggestions for use. You'll need a little time to assemble the necessary materials and make the constructions, but with few exceptions, the projects can be completed in an evening.

Although you may want to explain how a game is played or how a moving part works, you'll find that most activities require little or no teacher direction or supervision. They are ideal for learning centers, and often constitute a learning center in themselves. The children can play on their own or with each other, using the games and activities to enrich their free time.

Learning Content

These hands-on activities span the major subject areas for the primary grades. Some constructions help introduce concepts, others provide practice in an enjoyable way. Still others, the props in particular, promote social interaction and encourage children to explore life skills in their imaginative play.

In addition, a number of constructions are designed to involve children in certain aspects of classroom management, such as taking attendance, recording assignments, and allocating classroom jobs. Children are happy to share responsibility when these routine tasks undergo some creative restructuring. What child wouldn't look forward to taking attendance if it involves parking toy cars or handing a train ticket to a conductor?

Although each construction is designed for a specific activity or application, the formats are very versatile. In some instances, a single construction can be used to teach more than one concept. For example, the Color Clown can teach number words as well as color words, and the Sticker Flash Cards can feature picture words as well as number sets. Other constructions have changeable formats. For example, if bulletin board space is limited, you can convert an activity to a flannel board game, using the same themes and patterns. Likewise, the components of a flannel board game can be enlarged for a bulletin board for group play. You and your students can make a regular activity of generating your own ways to use these materials.

Specific concepts and skills featured in **Hands-On Patterns and Props** include:

Language Arts. Reading vocabulary, vowel sounds, hard and soft consonant sounds, alphabetizing, language development
Mathematics. Counting, reading number words, addition and subtraction facts, reading and telling time, weighing and measuring
Science. Collecting and classifying, body parts, constellations, metamorphosis, seasons
Social Studies. Map reading, time zones
Art. Color words, color mixing, life drawing

Materials for Construction

Most of the constructions require materials and equipment already available to you at school. Others require some saving or recycling, and occasionally you may need to make a small purchase at a stationery or variety store. All the items and quantities you need are listed at the beginning of every project. For your reference, here is a list of materials and tools most frequently called for:

brass fasteners	cardboard
clear contact paper	construction paper
felt	flannel
hole punch	markers
matte knife	opaque projector
paper clips	pins
rubber cement	shoe boxes
string	tape
tissue boxes	white glue
yarn	tempera paints

These items are less likely to be found in your school supply room, but they are easy to find:

canning jar lids and bands
canvas tarp or drop cloth
flashlight
self-stick labels
stickers

Homemade doesn't have to look homemade. When you use the patterns provided for each hands-on construction, your classroom displays can look as professional and inviting as any manufactured display. They can be as durable as well, if you use sturdy cardboard and take the time to laminate with clear contact paper.

With care in the construction and imagination in the application of these designs, you're sure to provide your students with a lot of learning fun.

Color Clown

Children match color words to correct colors.

OBJECTIVE: To reinforce color and color word recognition

LEVEL: 1 - 2

MATERIALS:
Color Clown and Balloon patterns
Opaque projector
Index cards, 3″ x 5″
Hole punch
Pins
Markers
Oaktag
Yarn
Colored construction paper

CONSTRUCTION:
1. Project clown pattern onto large piece of oaktag taped to a wall. Trace and cut out. Color with felt pens.
2. Staple clown to bulletin board.
3. Trace balloon pattern onto construction paper of colors to be learned. Attach a length of yarn in a matching color to each balloon.
4. Staple balloons to bulletin board, several above each hand of the clown. Gather the pieces of yarn in each group, tie together, and pin to clown's hands. Put a pin on each balloon to hold word card.
5. Write color words on index cards, with self-checking dots of color on back. Punch a hole at the top of each card. Store cards in a tissue box stapled to bottom of bulletin board.

ACTIVITY:
1. Each child takes a card, reads the word aloud, then hangs the card on the proper balloon.
2. When all balloons have been filled, reverse the process. Each child first reads the color name, then replaces the card in the box.

VARIATION:
● Make the clown out of heavy cardboard and use as a stand-up display with real balloons. Children match cards to colors.

Color Clown

Balloon

Keys to Letter Lockers

Children sort word keys into lockers labeled with hard and soft consonants.

OBJECTIVE: To discriminate hard and soft consonant sounds

LEVEL: 2 - 3

MATERIALS:
Consonant Keys pattern
Word lists for hard and soft consonant sounds
2 shoeboxes with lids
Oaktag strips
Hole punch
Marker
Rubber cement
Pins
Poster paints
Bulletin board letters

CONSTRUCTION:
1. Trace keys on oaktag and cut out. Make a square-headed key for each hard consonant word and a round-headed key for each soft consonant word.
2. Print one word from the word list on each key. Punch a hole in each key.
3. Paint shoeboxes to cover writing. Cut a keyhole in each box lid. Label each lid with a hard or soft consonant name, such as Carl and Cindy for hard and soft C. Glue a word list in the bottom of each shoebox.
4. Pin title to bulletin board. Staple shoeboxes vertically to bulletin board to resemble lockers. Place correct lid on each box. Hang the keys on pins along the bottom of the board.

ACTIVITY:
1. Child takes a key, reads the word, repeats the sound made by the initial consonant, and inserts key in appropriate keyhole.
2. After sorting all keys, child opens lockers and checks words against list inside, then corrects any mistakes.
3. Child closes lockers and hangs keys on pins in random order.

Keys to Letter Lockers

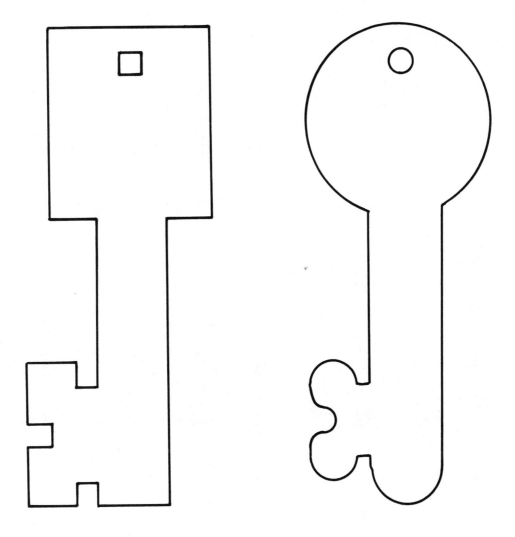

Keys to Letter Lockers

Hard C	Soft C
cake	cent
call	center
candy	celery
carrot	certain
class	Cindy
clap	cinder
coat	city
cold	cider
cup	cinnamon
come	ceiling

Hard G	Soft G
game	gem
girl	gym
goat	giraffe
gate	gentle
gift	gentleman
glove	germ
give	Germany
glass	Gerald
gold	gerbil
grape	general

Haunted House

Children match vowel sounds on word cards to sounds in words uttered by ghosts in this haunted house.

OBJECTIVE: To identify long and short vowel sounds

LEVEL: 1 - 3

MATERIALS:
Haunted House and Ghost patterns
Opaque projector
Construction paper (black, gray, white)
Black felt pen
Bulletin board letters
Index cards
Oaktag
Pins

CONSTRUCTION:
1. Project haunted house pattern onto black or gray construction paper. Trace and cut out. Cut slits for windows and doors. Fold out to make them open.
2. Trace and cut out ghosts and voice balloons from white construction paper. Outline with black felt pen. Write Halloween words on voice balloons.
3. Write matching words on index cards. Punch a hole in the top of each card.
4. Cut oaktag rectangle slightly larger than cards.
5. Staple the house on the bulletin board. Place a ghost and voice balloon in each window and door. Add a pin below each voice balloon. Staple bottom and sides of oaktag rectangle to lower corner of bulletin board. Store word cards here.
6. Pin on bulletin board letters to form title.

ACTIVITY:
1. Child takes a word card, reads the word aloud, then hangs it below the Halloween word with the same vowel sound. Child pronounces the vowel sound that is the same in both words.
2. When children have mastered these words, add new ones. You may also wish to change the words in the voice balloons.

Haunted House

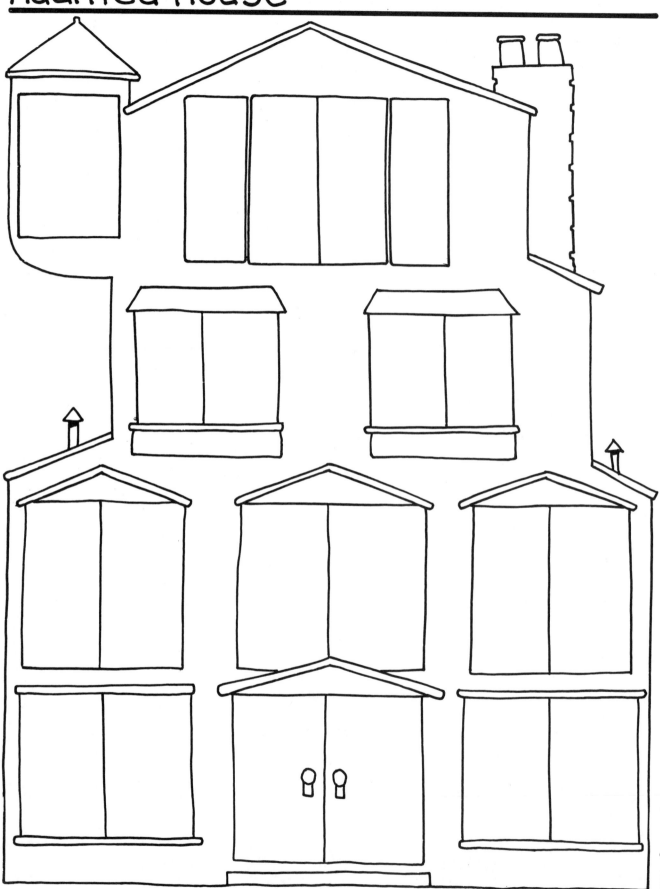

Haunted House

Halloween Words	Matching Words
bats	fast
cape	bake
skeleton	desk
Halloween	tree
witch	miss
night	time
goblin	doll
ghost	boat
pumpkin	duck
costume	tune

Bowling Board

Students knock down big bowling pins to demonstrate subtraction problems.

OBJECTIVE: To reinforce subtraction facts of 10

LEVEL: 1 - 3

MATERIALS:
Bowling Ball and Pin patterns
Large sheet of white poster board
3 large sheets of black poster board
White crayon
Brass fasteners
Bulletin board letters
Tissue box

CONSTRUCTION:
1. Trace and cut out 10 bowling pins from white poster board.
2. Tape 2 pieces of black poster board together. Arrange bowling pins in a pyramid. Attach pins to poster board with brass fasteners. Staple to bulletin board.
3. Cut out 11 balls from black poster board. Write subtraction facts of 10, without answers, on the front in white crayon. Write answers on the back.
4. Staple tissue box below the bowling pins. Place balls with subtraction problems into this holder.
5. Pin on bulletin board letters for title.

ACTIVITY:
1. Each child takes a number fact ball from the holder. He or she knocks down the number of pins to be subtracted from 10 as stated in the equation. The child says the complete equation, including the answer.
2. Children check their answers by counting the number of pins left upright. This number must match the number on the back of the bowling ball.

VARIATION:
● The same setup can be used for other number facts. Change the number of pins to fit the facts used. Addition can be performed by starting with all the pins down at first.

Bowling Board

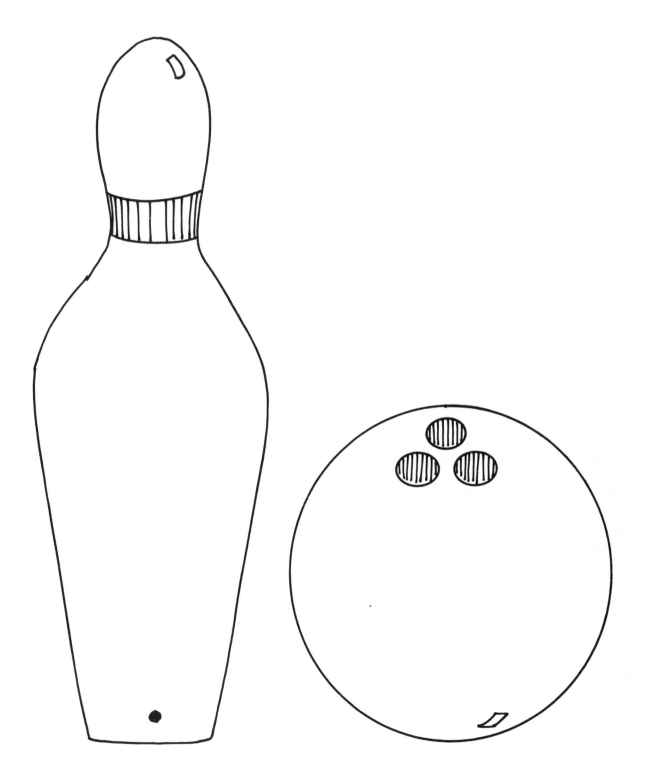

19

Monkey in the Middle

Children must put the correct missing number on the monkey in the middle of an addition equation.

OBJECTIVE: To reinforce addition and subtraction skills by finding missing numbers

LEVEL: 1 - 3

MATERIALS:
Monkey, Gymsuit, Square patterns
Construction paper (brown and a contrasting color)
Markers
Opaque projector
Tissue box or large envelope
Pins
Bulletin board letters
Monkey in the Middle worksheet

CONSTRUCTION:
1. Hang up both sheets of construction paper on a wall. Project patterns at 200%. Trace monkey on brown 3 times, gymsuit on contrasting color 3 times, square one time (becomes a pattern). Cut out all figures.
2. Trace and cut 23 squares out of colored paper. Print numbers on cards, two of each from 0 to 9, three 10's. Punch a hole in the top of each card.
3. Paste gymsuits on monkeys. Paste a number 10 on one gymsuit.
4. Match up squares so that each pair adds up to ten. On the back of each pair of cards put matching colored dots as a self-checking mechanism.
5. Pin title letters on bulletin board. Staple on one unnumbered monkey, a plus sign, the other unnumbered monkey, an equal sign, and the numbered monkey. Place pins on chests of unnumbered monkeys to hold number cards.
6. Staple empty tissue box to bottom of bulletin board. Add number cards.

ACTIVITY:
1. Child hangs any number on first monkey, then finds the correct number to hang on the second monkey. To check answer, child looks for matching color dots on back of cards.
2. Duplicate and distribute copies of the accompanying worksheet. Children fill in missing numbers to review addition facts.

Monkey, Gymsuit, Square

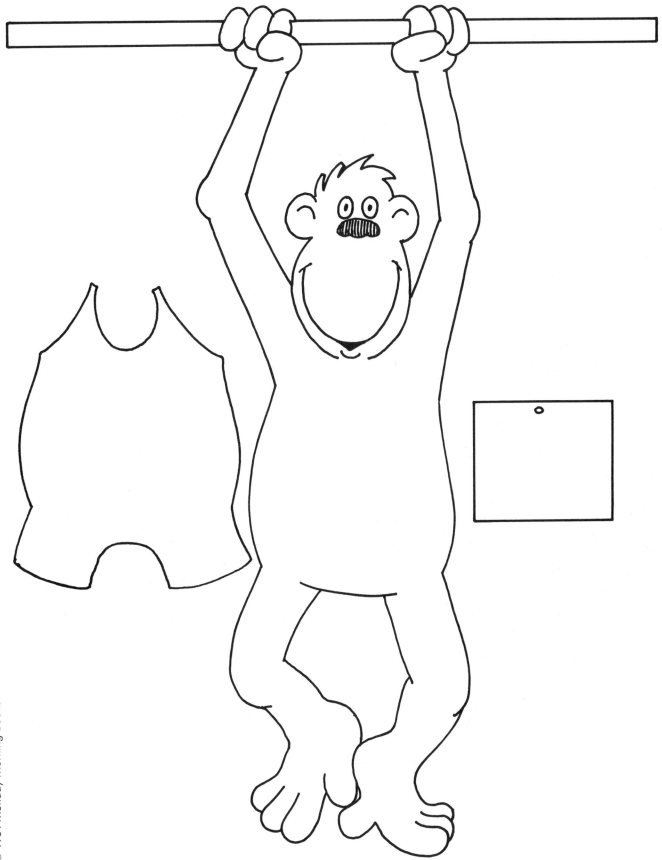

Monkey in the Middle

The monkey in the middle needs a number. What number will make each fact correct?

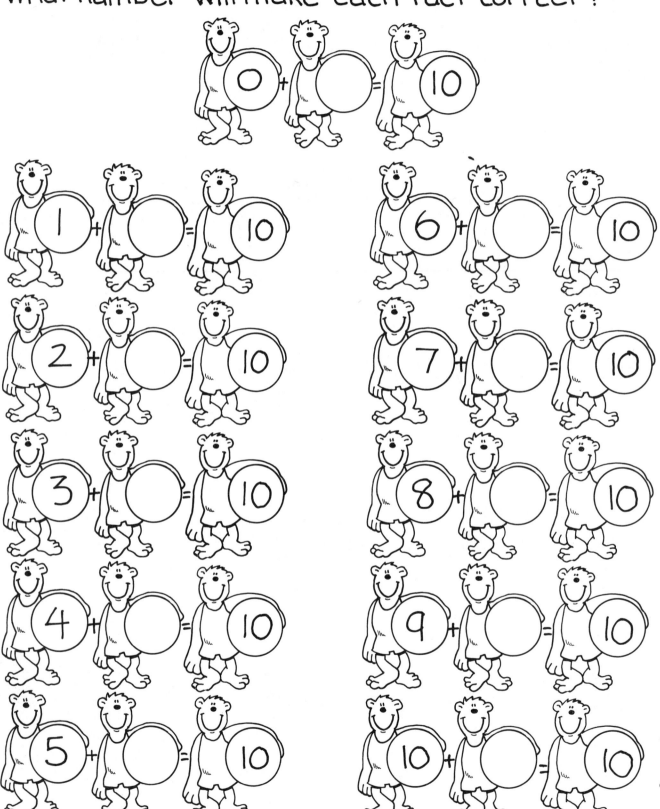

0 + ◯ = 10

1 + ◯ = 10   6 + ◯ = 10

2 + ◯ = 10   7 + ◯ = 10

3 + ◯ = 10   8 + ◯ = 10

4 + ◯ = 10   9 + ◯ = 10

5 + ◯ = 10   10 + ◯ = 10

Spice Up the ABC's

Children arrange spice bottles in alphabetical order.

OBJECTIVE: To reinforce alphabetizing skill

LEVEL: 2 - 3

MATERIALS:
3 shoeboxes with lids
Spice labels
26 empty small containers (such as vitamin bottles)
Rubber cement, paste, or glue
Bulletin board letters

CONSTRUCTION:
1. Duplicate and cut out spice labels. Notice that there are no herbs or spices that begin with the letters E, I, J, K, Q, U, X, Y, Z. If you want students to sequence the entire alphabet, have them make up humorous names beginning with these letters and write them on the blank labels.
2. Glue a label on each empty container.
3. Pin letters on bulletin board to form title.
4. Staple shoebox bottoms beneath title to form shelves. Staple lids along bottom of bulletin board with edges up to form lip. Place spice bottles on this ledge in random order.
5. Add labels A - I, J - R, S - Z to three shoebox shelves if your students need these hints.
6. Store bottles in shoeboxes when you take down this display.

ACTIVITY:
1. Arrange spice bottles on shoebox shelves, leaving out a few letters. Child replaces remaining bottles in correct alphabetical order.
2. For more challenge, leave one shelf of bottles for child to put back in order.
3. Eventually each student should be able to place all spice bottles on the shelves in correct alphabetical order.

Spice Up the ABC's

ALLSPICE	BASIL	CURRY POWDER
DILL	FENNEL	GINGER
HORSE-RADISH	LEMON BALM	MARJORAM
NUTMEG	OREGANO	PAPRIKA
ROSEMARY	SAGE	TARRAGON
VERBENA	WATERCRESS	

© 1984 Monday Morning Books

Monkey Mobiles

Numbered monkeys swing by their tails on mobiles that children color and lace together themselves.

OBJECTIVE: To reinforce number sequencing skills

LEVEL: K - 1

MATERIALS:
Monkey Cards pattern
Crayons
Yarn
String or cord
Hole punches
Cellophane tape

CONSTRUCTION:
1. Duplicate a set of monkey cards for each child.
2. Cut 2 pieces of yarn for each child. The first should be about 6 inches long, the second about 4 feet long.
3. Wrap a small piece of cellophane tape around one end of each piece of yarn to make threading easier.
4. Hang a length of string or cord about four feet high across a corner of the room.

ACTIVITY:
1. Give each child a set of cards, some crayons, and 2 pieces of yarn. Have children color in their monkey cards. Help them punch holes in cards.
2. Help children thread the end of the small piece of yarn through the holes on trapeze of the first monkey card. Then tie ends to form a loop.
3. Show children how to tie the untaped end of the long piece of yarn to the back of the loop.
4. Children lace together the monkey cards in sequence, threading yarn up through the bottom of one monkey and down through the hand on the next monkey. Knot the yarn and leave it dangling below the last monkey.
5. Clip or tie monkey mobiles to suspended cord. Have children stand in front of their mobiles and count to 10.
6. Display mobiles for awhile, then give them to the children to take home.

Monkey Mobiles

Monkey Mobiles

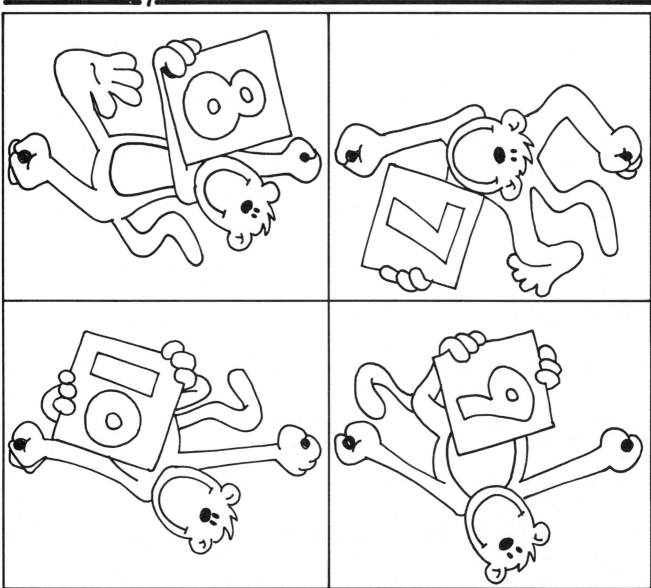

Figure Skater

Children practice writing numerals on laminated cards, then in a "skating rink" filled with salt or sand.

OBJECTIVE: To practice forming numerals correctly

LEVEL: K - 1

MATERIALS:
Figure Skater pattern and cards
Sturdy shallow box
Clear contact paper
Pocket folder
Grease pencil
Piece of cloth
Unsharpened pencil with eraser
Thumbtack
Salt or sand

CONSTRUCTION:
1. Duplicate cards on heavy paper and laminate with contact paper.
2. Store cards on one side of pocket folder, grease pencil and cloth square on other side.
3. Duplicate figure skater on oaktag, color, and cut out. Fold on dotted lines, then tack tabs to pencil eraser.
4. Fill bottom of box with an inch of salt or sand. Stand pencil in box.
5. Place folder and box skating rink at a learning station.

ACTIVITY:
1. The child traces numerals on cards with grease pencil.
2. Next he or she uses the figure skater pencil to form figures inside the rink.
3. After practicing figures on cards and in rink, the child may try writing numerals on unlined paper. He or she should sign the paper and leave it in the back of the folder for teacher to check.
4. Before leaving the learning station, the child must wipe markings off laminated cards and smooth the salt or sand in the rink.

Figure Skater

Figure Skating

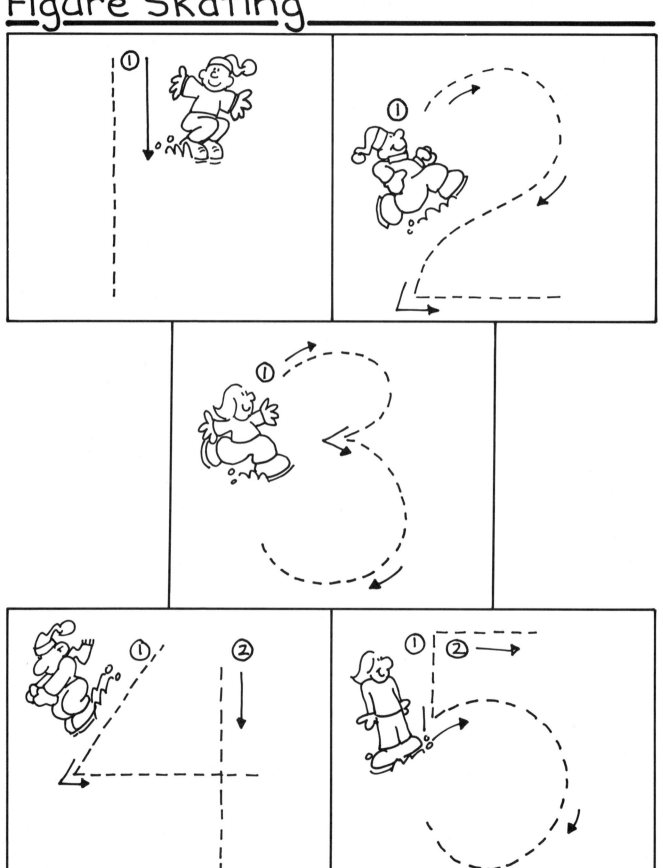

Figure Skating

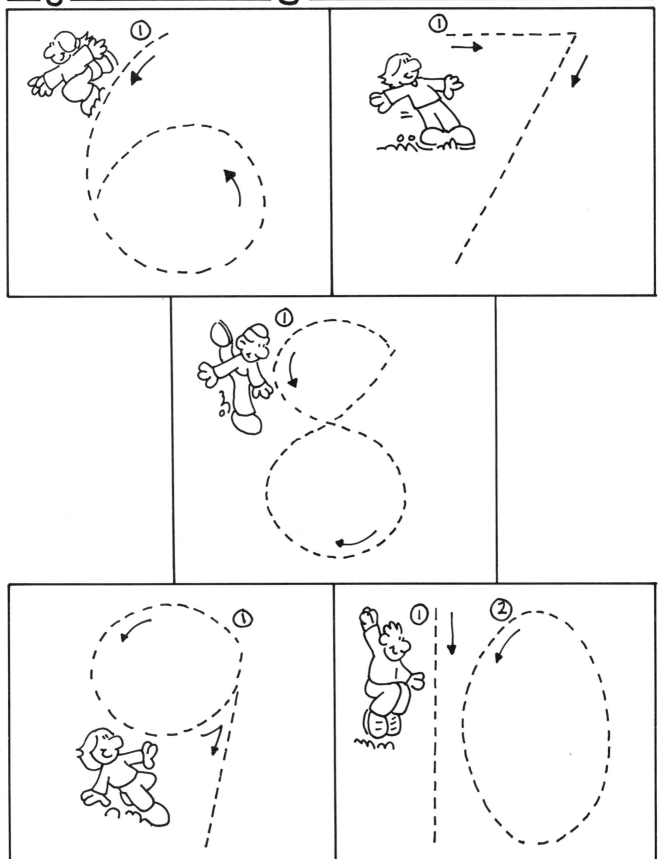

Sticker Flash Cards

Colorful stickers become a self-checking device on flash cards to teach number recognition.

OBJECTIVE: To reinforce number - quantity associations

LEVEL: K - 2

MATERIALS:
Ruled index cards
Small stickers

CONSTRUCTION:
1. To make cards for nonreaders, print a large numeral on the ruled side of an index card. Place the same number of identical stickers on the unruled side.
2. To make cards for readers, print the numeral on the left of the ruled side and place the same number of identical stickers on the right. Print the number word on the back. (For larger numbers, you may wish to group the small stickers by fives or tens.)
3. Stack nonreader cards with numeral side up. Stack reader cards with word side up.

ACTIVITY:
1. Have child look at each card, then say the number or word. Child turns card over to check answer.
2. After several times, shuffle cards so that numbers are in random order. Have child read cards again and check any uncertain or incorrect answers.

VARIATION:

● Make sticker flash cards for reading simple words. Print a word on ruled side, place corresponding sticker on unruled side. Child reads words, checks answers with sticker pictures.

Time in a Line

Children practice reading and telling time on clocks hung in a line.

OBJECTIVE: To reinforce time-telling by the hour, half-hour, and quarter-hour

LEVEL: 1 - 3

MATERIALS:
Clock pattern
Paper clips
Black marker
Clothesline
Spring-type clothespins
Paper plates
Index cards (3″ x 5″)
Rubber cement
Tissue box or envelope

CONSTRUCTION:
1. Duplicate clock patterns. Cut out and glue on paper plates.
2. Draw hands on the clocks so that each tells a different time. Write the time on the back for a self-check. Punch a hole at the bottom of the clock.
3. Unfold paper clips and hook onto paper plate clocks.
4. Hang a clothesline across one side of the room. Pin each clock to the line in time sequence.
5. Write times on index cards. Punch a hole at the top of each card.
6. Place cards in tissue box or envelope on a table beneath the clothesline.

ACTIVITY:
1. Child picks a time card from the box and hooks it on the clock that it matches. Child checks answer by comparing card to time written on the back of the clock.
2. For beginners, start with hour clocks. Use the half-hour and quarter-hour clocks for more skilled time tellers. Begin with the clocks in time sequence. Mix them up later on for more challenge.

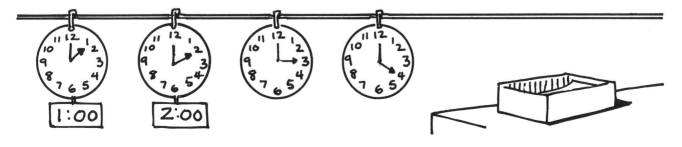

Time in a Line

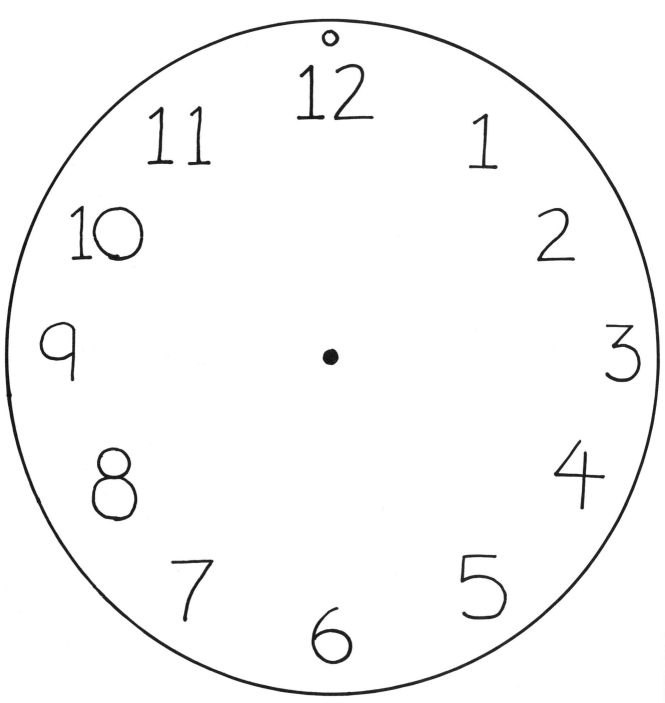

Egg Scale and Ruler

Children first paint faces on hardboiled eggs, then weigh and measure them as if they were patients in a doctor's office.

OBJECTIVE: To reinforce measurement skills

LEVEL: 2 and up

MATERIALS:
Egg Activity patterns
Egg Weight and Height Chart
Hardboiled eggs of varying sizes, one for each child
Markers
Small platform scale that measures ounces
Egg carton
Small wood block
Rubber cement
Poster board

CONSTRUCTION:
1. Let each child decorate an egg to create an egg patient a day or two before doing this activity.
2. Cut two compartments out of egg carton. Glue one to the platform of the scale. Glue the other onto the block. Reset the scale to 0.
3. Duplicate egg ruler. Glue on poster board and cut out. Glue ruler to block directly behind egg cup so that it can measure height of eggs.
4. Duplicate egg weights reference card. Mount on poster board and cut out.
5. Duplicate Egg Weight and Height Chart.

ACTIVITY:
1. Have children list the names of their egg patients on the Egg Weight and Height Chart.
2. Children take turns weighing and measuring their eggs, then entering the data on the chart.
3. Have children sort eggs into weight groups. Ask if weight always corresponds to height.

Egg Scale and Ruler

EGG WEIGHTS

small... 2oz.

medium... 2¼oz.

large... 2½oz.

extra large... 2¾oz

jumbo... 3oz.

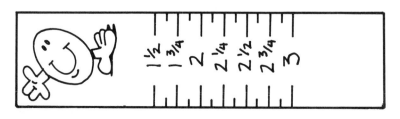

Egg Weight and Height Chart

NAME OF PATIENT	OUNCES	INCHES	NAME OF PATIENT	OUNCES	INCHES

Blackboard Backboard

In this basketball game, players must correctly add or multiply chalkboard numbers hit with a sponge.

OBJECTIVE: To reinforce number facts in various operations

LEVEL: 3 and up

MATERIALS:
Wastebasket(s)
Masking tape
Kitchen sponges

CONSTRUCTION:
1. Draw a large 3 x 3 grid on the board. Write a number in each box. For more advanced students, use fractions, two-digit numbers, and zero.
2. Put wastebasket directly below grid. More wastebaskets may be added to use the grid more fully.
3. Place long strip of masking tape on floor 3 - 5 feet away from wastebasket(s).

ACTIVITY:
1. Divide class into 2 teams, lined up on either side of classroom.
2. Teams alternate sending player to line to throw sponges against numbers on the blackboard. Sponges should be aimed so they land in the wastebasket for a point.
3. Player must correctly add or multiply numbers hit by sponges and try to get sponges to land in basket. Score 2 points for correct answer and a basket, 1 point for either correct answer or basket.
4. For less competitive game, let team members assist with the answers to the math problems.

40

Snail Trails

Three snails leave primary color trails that cross to produce secondary colors.

OBJECTIVE: To reinforce primary colors and discover secondary colors

LEVEL: K - 3

MATERIALS:
Snail pattern
Red, yellow, blue construction paper
Black marker
Large sheet of butcher paper or newsprint
Small pieces of sponge for dab-painting
Red, yellow, blue tempera paints
Snail Trail worksheet

CONSTRUCTION:
1. Trace and cut out a snail in each primary color. Label snails with their color names.
2. Cut a large piece of paper for each child. Staple snails far apart on each piece, facing edges.
3. Prepare a container of each primary color with a sponge for each child.

ACTIVITY:
1. Work with 3 or 4 children at a time. Give each child a large snail paper, 3 containers of paint, and 3 sponges.
2. Have each child dab a red trail behind the red snail. As red dries, have child start a yellow trail behind the yellow snail. This trail should cross the red trail at least once.
3. As yellow dries, have child start a blue trail behind the blue snail, crossing both red and yellow snail trails. Stop dabbing when trails have crossed several times. Have children tell what color they see at the crossings. If they do not know, name the secondary colors for them. Label crossings with color names.
4. Display children's work in the classroom. Refer to it from time to time to review primary and secondary colors.
5. You may wish to follow this activity with the Snail Trail Worksheet, page 45.

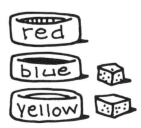

Snail Trails

Snail Trails

Color each snail. Color the trail behind each snail the same color as the snail. Watch what happens when the snails cross paths.

Use 3 colors to make 6 colors.

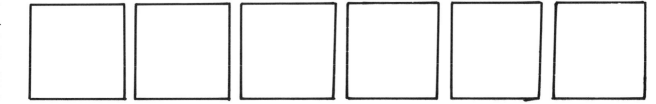

Self-Portraits

Children frame and display paintings of themselves.

OBJECTIVE: To build self-esteem

LEVEL: K - 3

MATERIALS:
Portrait Frame pattern
Poster board in different colors
White drawing or watercolor paper
Rubber cement
Glue-on picture hooks
Exacto knife
Tempera paints and brushes, drawing pencils, or felt pens
Mirrors
Cardboard easels (optional)

CONSTRUCTION:
1. To make a frame for each child, trace frame pattern twice on poster board and cut out. With exacto knife, cut out oval from one frame, leaving other one whole for backing.
2. Trace oval shape on drawing paper for each student. Students will do self-portraits inside ovals.
3. If desired, make desk-top easels out of corrugated cardboard and shoe boxes. See diagram on page 48.
4. Set up art materials and mirrors for students.

ACTIVITY:
1. Have children sketch or paint their self-portraits in the ovals on the drawing paper. They may need to check in the mirror to get details correct.
2. Help children slip finished self-portraits between the oval frame and its backing. Glue together with rubber cement.
3. Glue hooks on back of frames. Display self-portraits in the classroom before letting children take them home.

Self-Portraits

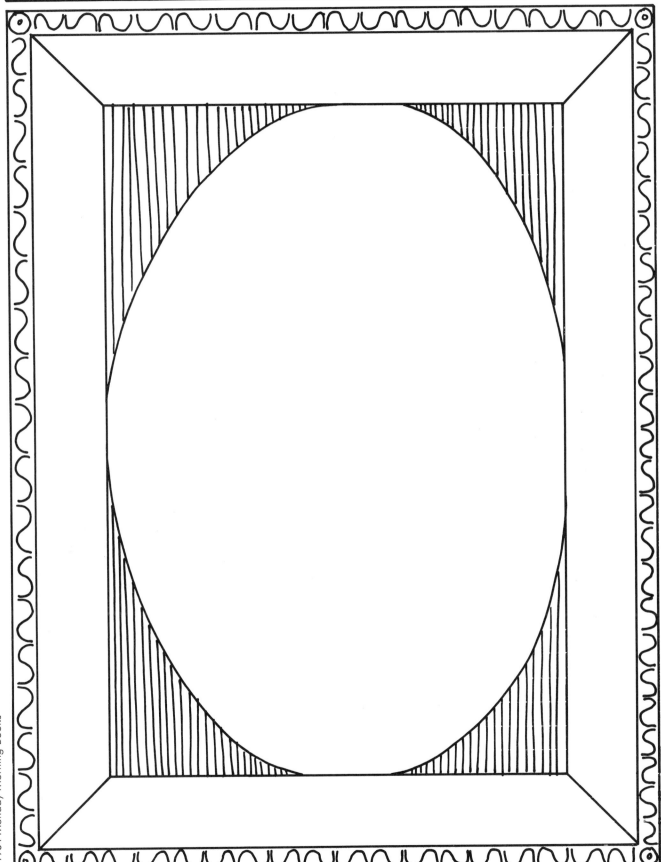

Self-Portraits

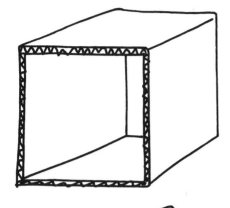

First cut off two facing panels.

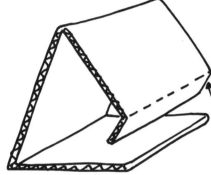

Then cut off another panel, and fold the remaining panel in 3 inches from bottom.

Shoebox holder

Glue shoebox holder to folded panel and bottom panel.

Science

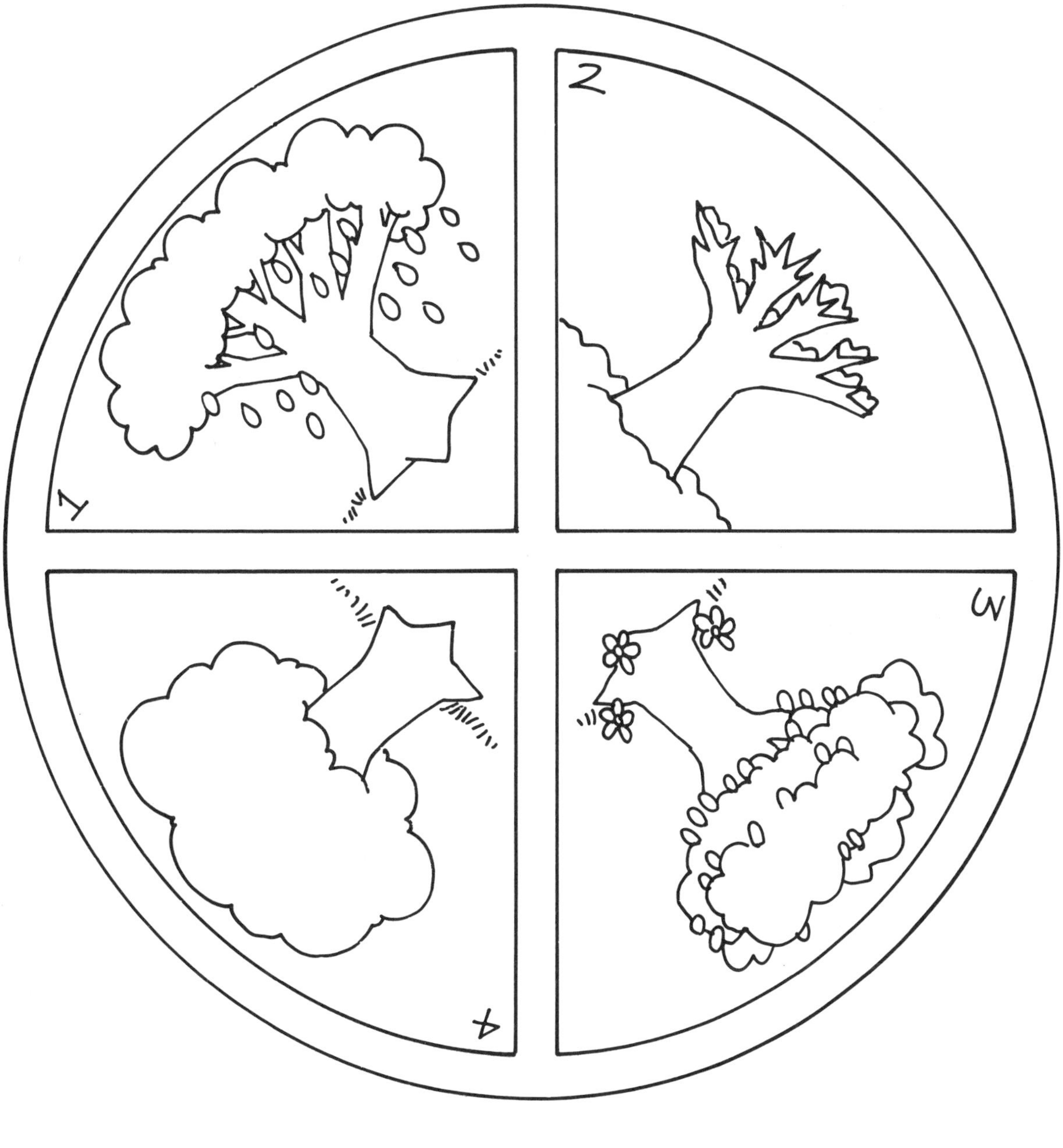

Body Puzzle

Young children learn the names of body parts while putting together a life-size puzzle.

OBJECTIVE: To learn the main parts of the body

LEVEL: Preschool - 2

MATERIALS:
Body Parts pattern
Opaque projector
2 large pieces of white poster board
Black marker
Large plastic bag
Clear contact paper
Canvas or other sturdy, solid color fabric

CONSTRUCTION:
1. Hang canvas on wall. Project body parts pattern onto canvas. Trace outline with black marker. Do not draw in lines dividing parts.
2. Hang 2 pieces of poster board on wall. Project body parts pattern and trace.
3. Cut out body parts and laminate with clear contact paper.
4. Roll up canvas. Store canvas and body parts in large plastic bag.

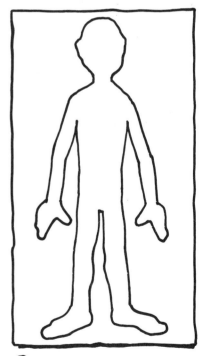

ACTIVITY:
1. Discuss with children the main parts of the body. Have children note the parts of their own bodies and where they are.
2. Show children the whole body drawn on canvas. Put the canvas on the floor. Take body parts out of bag one by one, have children identify them, and tell where to place them on the whole body.
3. When children are familiar with the parts and can place them correctly, make the body puzzle available for a free time activity. At the end of play, children should put all body parts and canvas mat back in the plastic bag.

Body Puzzle

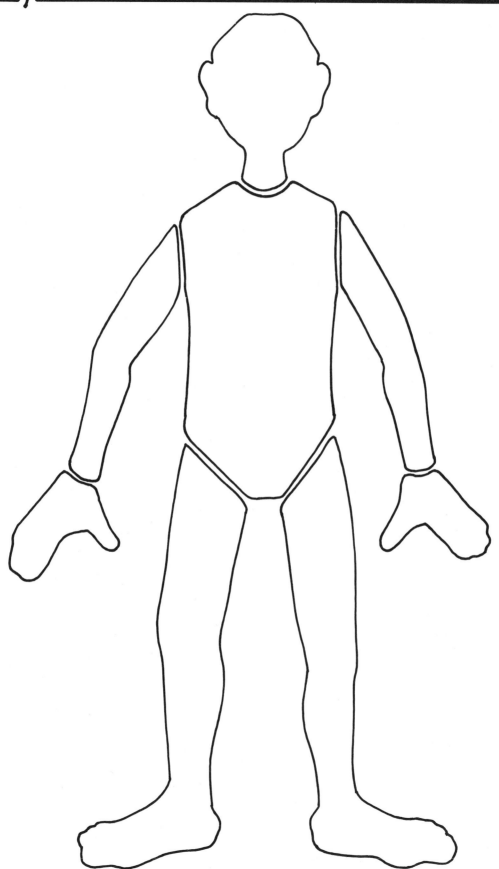

Day and Night

Children open shutters on a day or night sky. They choose correct figures to add to it.

OBJECTIVE: To reinforce the concept of night and day

LEVEL: Preschool - 1

MATERIALS:
Day and Night patterns
Large flat box with lid
2 pieces of poster board same size as box
4 narrow strips of oaktag
Light and dark blue flannel or felt
White glue
Felt scraps in assorted colors
Black marker
Clear plastic mending tape
Zip lock bag

CONSTRUCTION:
1. Cover one piece of poster board with flannel or felt, light blue on one side, dark blue on the other.
2. Glue narrow oaktag strips to each side to create illusion of four window panes. Place this "night and day" panel in bottom of box.
3. Cut other piece of poster board in half lengthwise to make 2 shutters. Draw designs on these, if you like.
4. Tape shutters to long edges of box. Put tape on both inside and outside of shutters to make very sturdy hinges.
5. Trace patterns onto felt scraps and cut out. Label, if desired, and store in zip lock bag inside box. Replace box lid.

ACTIVITY:
1. Child opens box, removes bag, and opens shutters to find either night or day.
2. Child sorts felt shapes and places correct object in each window pane. Then child turns panel over and places remaining shapes on the other side.
3. Follow up this activity with a discussion about night and day. Ask children what they can see and do during each time.

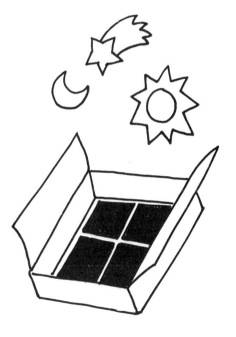

Day and Night

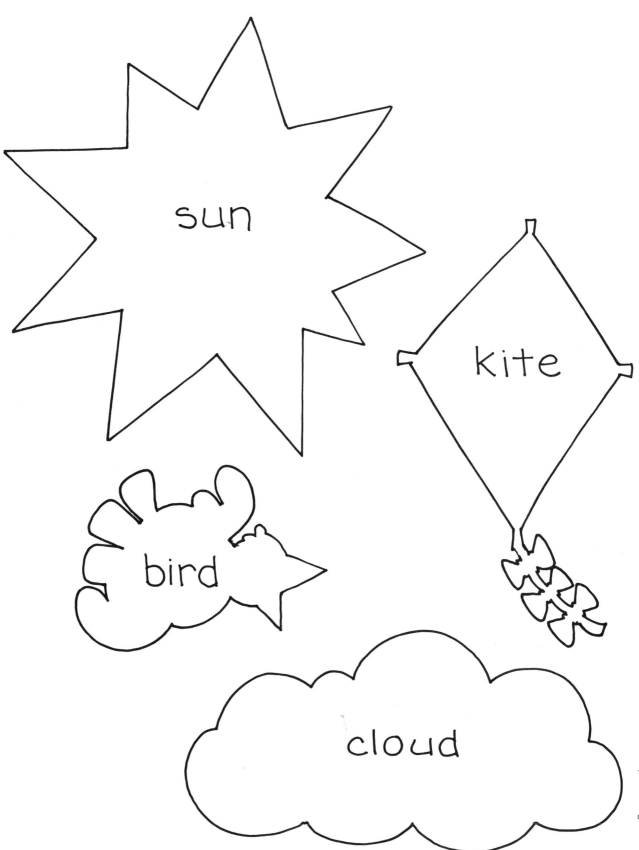

sun

kite

bird

cloud

Day and Night

Metamorphosis Story Disks

This viewing device shows frog and butterfly development and changing seasons.

OBJECTIVE: To foster sequencing skills

LEVEL: K - 3

MATERIALS:
Metamorphosis Paddle and Picture Disk patterns
Cardboard or poster board
Colored markers or watercolors
Paste
3 brass fasteners
Black marker

CONSTRUCTION:
1. Color in 3 story disks.
2. Cut out story disks and paddle pattern. Cut out window in paddle pattern.
3. Trace paddle onto cardboard or poster board 3 times and cut out.
4. Paste story disks on cardboard or poster board, then cut them out.
5. Place a paddle over each story disk. Attach with brass fastener through dots.
6. Label each paddle with title of picture lesson.

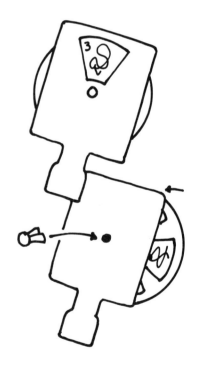

ACTIVITY:
1. Child holds paddle in one hand and turns picture disk with the other. Color pictures appear in sequence through the window.
2. Have child explain what is happening in each picture in correct sequence.
3. When child is fairly familiar with the sequences, have him or her anticipate and tell the next sequence before turning the disk. You can also do the reverse, by asking what happened in the preceding picture.

Metamorphosis Paddle

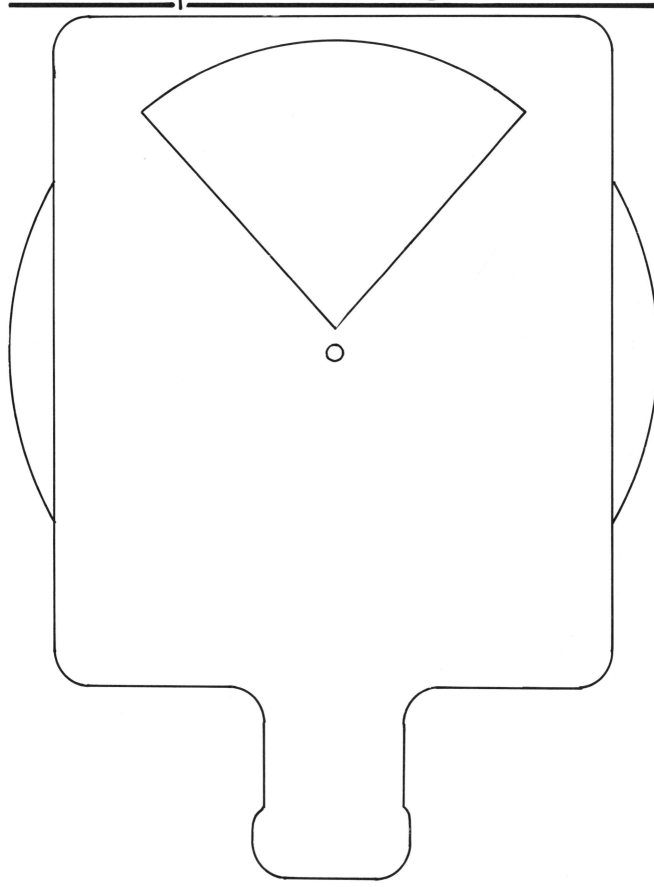

Metamorphosis Picture Disk

The Changing of the Seasons

Metamorphosis Picture Disk

Frog Metamorphosis

Metamorphosis Picture Disk

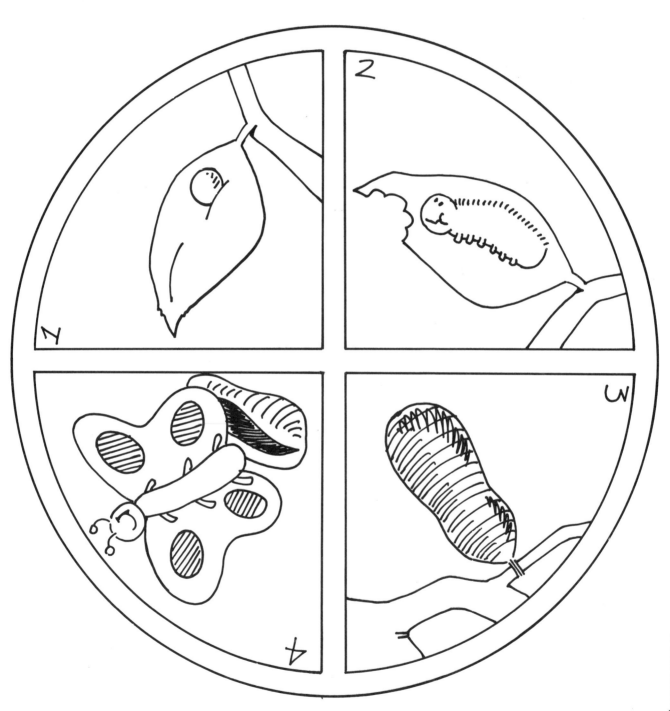

Butterfly Metamorphosis

Flashlight Planetarium

Children learn to identify constellations in the classroom using flashlights and stencils.

OBJECTIVE: To learn to identify constellation patterns

LEVEL: 3 and up

MATERIALS:
Constellation Stencils
Constellation Configuration cards
Canning jar lids and bands
Hammer and nail
Wood block
Glue
Flashlight

CONSTRUCTION:
1. Cut out constellation stencils.
2. Tape each stencil to a lid. Put lid on wood block and hammer nail through each black dot to pierce lid. Older students might enjoy doing this.
3. Glue each lid inside a ring.
4. Duplicate constellation cards for reference.

ACTIVITY:
1. Child holds flashlight upright with lid on top of lens. Child turns on flashlight to reveal the constellation pattern as points of light.
2. Child finds and names star pattern on constellation cards. Child repeats procedure until all constellations in the personal planetarium have been viewed.

canning jar lid

Constellation Stencils

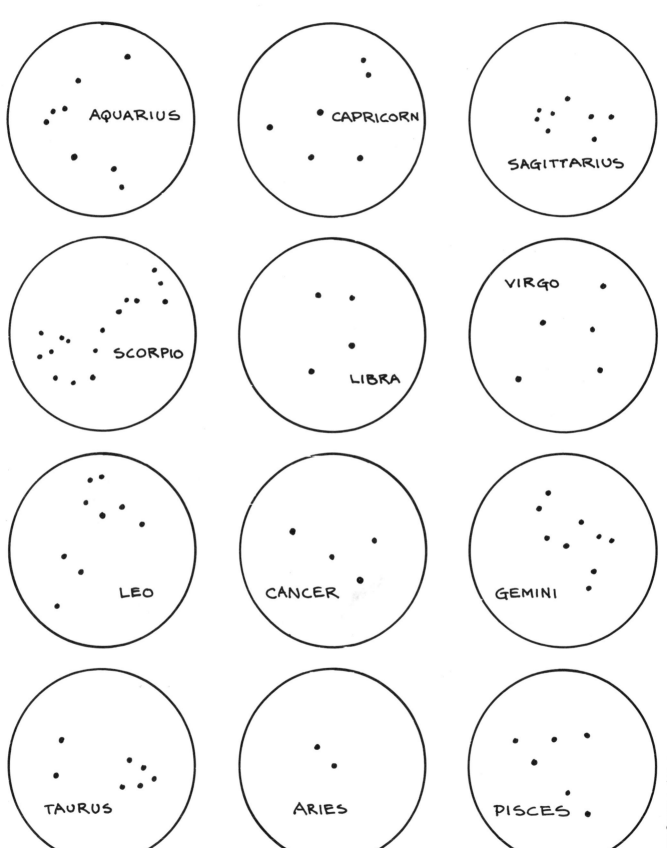

AQUARIUS

CAPRICORN

SAGITTARIUS

SCORPIO

LIBRA

VIRGO

LEO

CANCER

GEMINI

TAURUS

ARIES

PISCES

Constellation Stencils

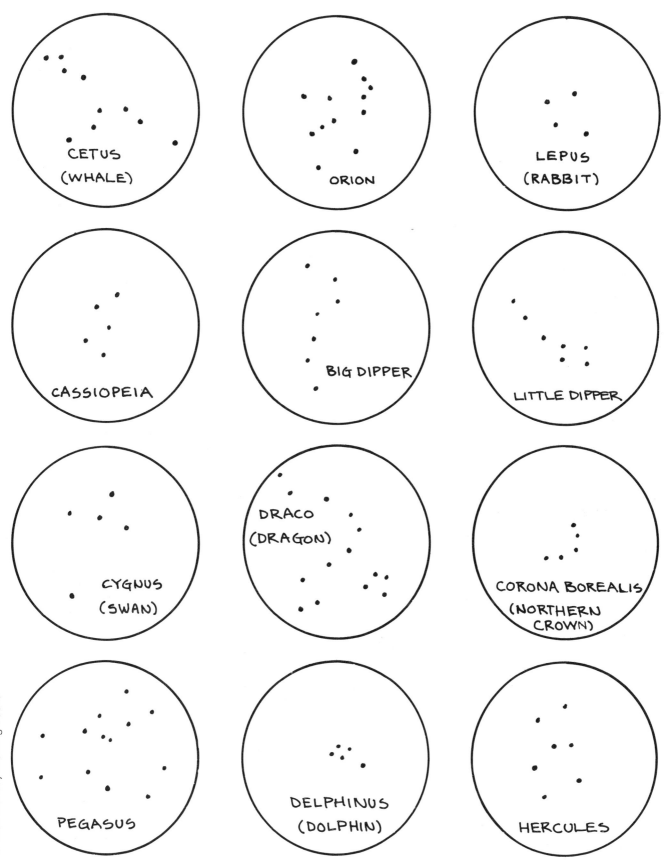

CETUS
(WHALE)

ORION

LEPUS
(RABBIT)

CASSIOPEIA

BIG DIPPER

LITTLE DIPPER

CYGNUS
(SWAN)

DRACO
(DRAGON)

CORONA BOREALIS
(NORTHERN
CROWN)

PEGASUS

DELPHINUS
(DOLPHIN)

HERCULES

Constellation Configurations

AQUARIUS

CAPRICORN

SAGITTARIUS

SCORPIO

LIBRA

VIRGO

LEO

CANCER

GEMINI

TAURUS

ARIES

PISCES

© 1984 Monday Morning Books

Constellation Configurations

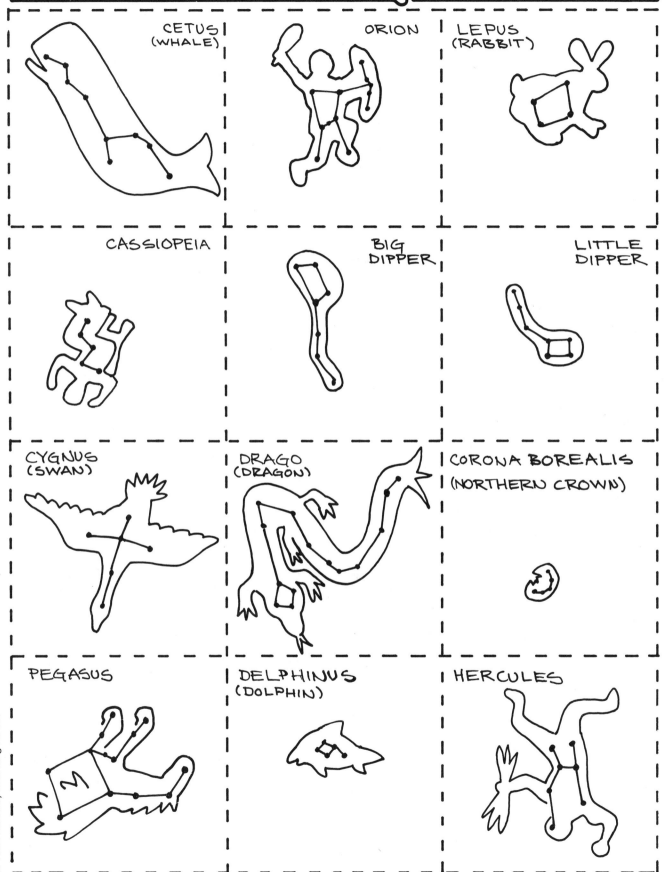

CETUS
(WHALE)

ORION

LEPUS
(RABBIT)

CASSIOPEIA

BIG
DIPPER

LITTLE
DIPPER

CYGNUS
(SWAN)

DRAGO
(DRAGON)

CORONA BOREALIS
(NORTHERN CROWN)

PEGASUS

DELPHINUS
(DOLPHIN)

HERCULES

Shirtbox Showcase

These boxes enable children to display their collections on a counter, table top, or bulletin board.

OBJECTIVE: To reinforce information learned in science lessons

LEVEL: 1 - 3 and up

MATERIALS:
Large shirtboxes with lids
Index cards
White glue
Plastic wrap
Tape or putty (optional)
Thumbtacks (optional)

CONSTRUCTION:
1. Cut out the middle of the shirtbox lid, leaving a half-inch margin all the way around as a frame.
2. Squeeze out a bead of glue along the inside of the frame. Stretch a piece of plastic wrap across frame and press in place. Trim away excess plastic.

ACTIVITY:
1. Children gather materials to make displays. Examples: rocks, fossils, leaves, flowers, shells, pictures of animals or their habitats.
2. Have children glue or tape items to bottom of box. Items can also be stuck on with putty so that they can be removed unharmed.
3. Show children how to label displays with index cards. Mount cards inside boxes with exhibited items.
4. Tack shirtbox bottoms to bulletin board or lay them on a flat surface for display. Place frames over boxes to protect them.

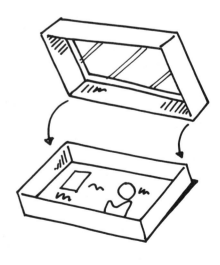

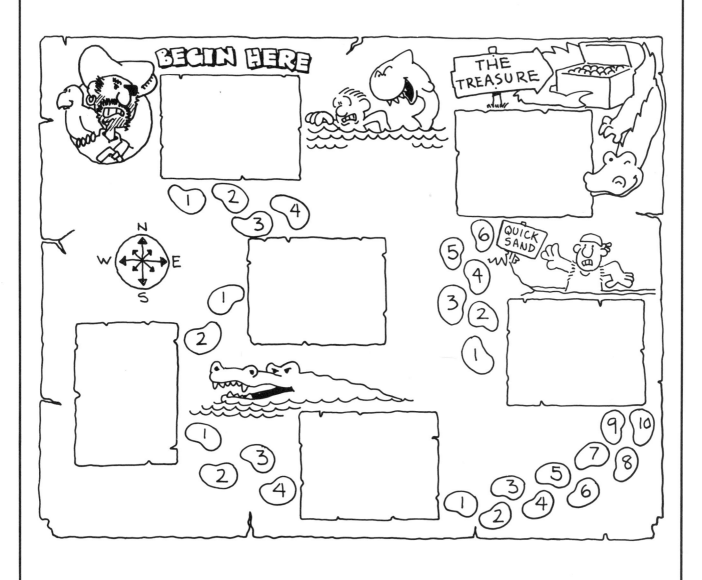

Town and Country Map

Children follow directions to drive toy cars from place to place on this floor map.

OBJECTIVE: To reinforce map reading skills

LEVEL: 1 - 3

MATERIALS:
Town and Country Map pattern
Opaque projector
Masking tape
White tarpaulin or canvas drop cloth (from paint store) cut 4' x 5'
Permanent black marker
Tempera paints and brushes
Acrylic sealant
Small toy cars and trucks
Direction cards
Oaktag

CONSTRUCTION:
1. Tape cloth to bare wall.
2. Project the image of the Town and Country map pattern at 500% onto the hanging cloth.
3. Trace the enlargement onto the fabric. You may want to use a second color marker for lettering street signs to make them stand out.
4. Spread map on floor and paint (or have students paint) in landmarks. Spray with acrylic sealant.
5. Duplicate direction cards on oaktag or card stock and cut apart.

ACTIVITY:
1. Place direction cards face down. Children choose a car or truck, pick a card and follow the directions.
2. Have older children use compass directions and make mileage estimates.
3. Encourage children to write out directions for others to follow.

Town and Country Map

ROUTE 1 (EAST-WEST)

TRAIN STATION

GAS

EAT

BIRD SANCTUARY

ROUTE 1 (NORTH-SOUTH)

SUNSET DRIVE

PICNIC GROVE

POND

PRODUCE STAND

Town and Country Map

ROUTE 1

MOVIE

MARKET

MAIN STREET

SCHOOL

LIBRARY →

CITY HALL

PLAYGROUND

APARTMENTS

ROUTE 201

N
W E
S

1 MILE

Town and Country Direction Cards

Turn right

Go to Main street.

Turn left.

Go to Route 201.

Go left 2 blocks.

Go to Route 1.

Go right 1 block.

Go north 3 blocks.

Town and Country Direction Cards

Go south
2 blocks.

Stop at
the library.

Go west
1 block.

Drive to the
movie theater.

Go east
2 blocks.

Buy groceries
at the market.

Go to the
train station.

Take family to
the playground.

Treasure Chest

A counting-steps map leads children to a hidden pirate chest filled with exciting treasures.

OBJECTIVE: To reinforce map reading skills

LEVEL: 2 - 3

MATERIALS:
Treasure Chest and Map patterns
2 small shoe boxes of identical size
Cardboard
Silver cloth tape or duct tape, at least 1" wide
Silver spray paint
Poster paints, beads, sequins, other decorations
White glue
Treasure Items (suggestions illustrated)

CONSTRUCTION:
1. Adjust length and width of pattern for decorative front panel to fit long side of shoe box.
2. Trace panel pattern onto cardboard and cut out. Also trace and cut out key, skull and crossbones.
3. Tape open boxes together lengthwise as shown to form inside hinge. Close boxes and tape together to form outside hinge.
4. Glue decorative panel to front of chest so that it is flush with top.
5. Spray chest silver. When dry, glue skull and crossbones to top. Paint or glue jewel-like details to front panel.
6. Fill treasure chest with costume jewelry and play money, then hide it.
7. Draw in the missing reference points on the treasure map so that directions will lead children to chest. Color and cut out the map. For more advanced children, write out a list of directions that lead to the treasure chest. Example: Take 8 steps to the library table, turn right. Directions should also use compass points.

ACTIVITY:
1. Give treasure map or list of directions to a small group of children and send them in search of treasure.
2. Encourage them to play act some of the adventures illustrated on the map as they follow the directions, counting their footsteps aloud.
3. Older students can hide the treasure and draw a map for others in the class to follow.

Treasure Chest

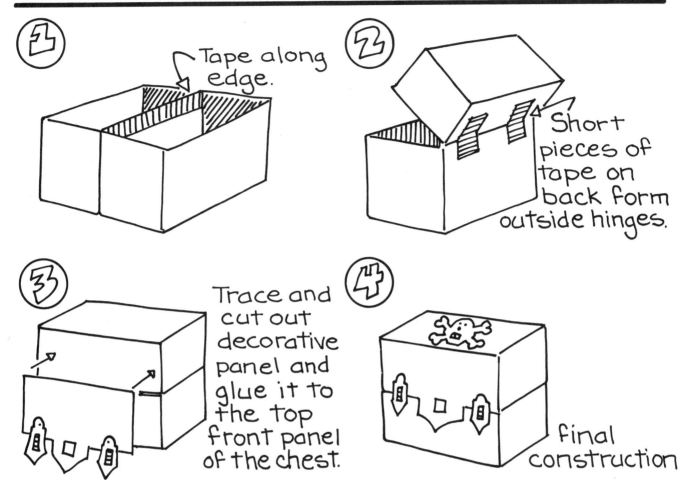

① Tape along edge.

② Short pieces of tape on back form outside hinges.

③ Trace and cut out decorative panel and glue it to the top front panel of the chest.

④ final construction

 painted poker chips

 shower curtain bead

 painted baby mug

 costume jewelry

Treasure Chest

Treasure Map

Time Zones

Traveling from one time zone to another and keeping track of the time is the challenge of this game.

OBJECTIVE: To reinforce the concept of time changes from one time zone to another

LEVEL: 3 and up

MATERIALS:
U.S. Time Zone Map
Opaque projector
Permanent black marker
White tarp or drop cloth
Watch pattern
Brass paper fasteners
U.S. Time Zone Activity Cards
Student atlases for reference
Oaktag

CONSTRUCTION:
1. Hang sturdy fabric on bare wall.
2. Project U.S. Time Zone Map and trace. Be sure to include state boundaries. Older students may enjoy helping with this work.
3. Duplicate watch pattern onto oaktag. Make enough copies for entire class.

ACTIVITY:
1. Rotate a globe to show students why there are time zones. Explain the concept of standard time and how time is calculated from the Prime Meridian in Greenwich, England.
2. Point out the 4 time zones in the continental United States. Review the names of the states in each time zone.
3. Distribute watch patterns. Have students cut out and decorate their watches, then attach hands with brass paper fasteners.
4. Lay the fabric time zone map on the floor. Have students gather around it. Then call on students one at a time to choose activity cards and walk from one city to another, setting their watches when they "leave" and resetting them when they "arrive." Students may use atlases or maps to locate cities and states. Reinforce U.S. geography facts by having students write more activity cards.

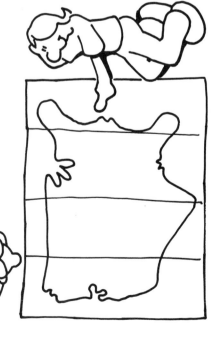

Time Zone Map

Watch

U.S. Time Zone Activity Cards

Cinderella has gone to a school dance in Arkansas. Her fairy godmother told her to be home by midnight or her dancing shoes will turn into muddy galoshes. Her fairy godmother forgot to set her watch when she flew in from Maryland. What time must Cinderella leave to avoid embarrassment in Arkansas?

You're standing on the eastern shore of Lake Michigan. It's noon. Look across the lake. What time is it on the western shore?

You're eating a bowl of cereal in California. It's 9 a.m. What might you be eating at this very moment if you lived in West Virginia?

The space shuttle is taking off from Cape Kennedy in Florida at 7 a.m. You live in northern Idaho. How early do you have to get up to watch the launch live on television?

It's election day, and the polls close in most states at 8 p.m. If it's 7 p.m. in Montana, can you still vote in South Carolina? In Oregon?

You return home to Iowa from a ski trip to Colorado, but you forget to reset your traveling alarm clock. The next morning the alarm rings and you get ready for school. Will you be on time? How early or late will you be?

It's your bedtime in Connecticut. If you were in Oregon, how much longer could you stay up?

You were born in Texas a few minutes before midnight on December 31, 1976. If you had been born the same exact moment in Rhode Island, in what year would you have been born?

You are flying from Maine to Arizona to visit the Grand Canyon. How far back should you set your watch before you land?

The Super Bowl is being played in California. You want to watch the live broadcast, which begins at 1 p.m. Pacific Time. You live in Alabama. What time should you turn on your television?

U.S. Time Zone Activity Cards

Your baby sister was born in Pennsylvania at 1 a.m., October 23. If she had been born in Nevada, what would be her time and date of birth?

You are a sheriff in Wyoming. You tell the Tennessee Troublemakers to be out of town by noon. They haven't reset their watches, however. If you have to chase them out of town, what time will their watches say?

Your big brother is at college in North Carolina. You're at home in Washington. He calls you at 8 a.m. his time. What are you doing?

You are flying across the country. You leave New York at 3 p.m. The flight takes 6 hours. What time is it in California when you land?

Your grandparents in New Mexico like to sleep late. It's 9 a.m. where you live in Virginia. Is it too early to give them a call? What time is it in New Mexico?

It's 7 p.m. at your house in Ohio. You're going to call your uncle in Colorado. What time does his watch show?

You live in New Hampshire. Your aunt from Oklahoma wrote to say she's coming to visit and will arrive at 5 p.m. You're not sure if she means her time or yours. When might she arrive?

It's 10 p.m. You're standing at the eastern edge of Wendover, Utah. What time is it at the other end of town, Wendover, Nevada?

The clock has just struck 12 on New Year's Eve at your house in New York. If you call your grandparents in Arizona to wish them happy new year, will they be celebrating too?

It's 6:05 p.m. at your house in Maryland. Your best friend gets home from school at 3:30 p.m. in California. Will your friend be home if you call right now?

Chicken
Fish
Meat
Spaghetti
Potatoes
Peas
Corn
Pie
Ice Cream

Contraction Cards

These cards fold to show how two words are shortened into one.

OBJECTIVE: To learn and reinforce the concept of contractions

LEVEL: 1 - 3

MATERIALS:
Contraction Cards
Strips of tagboard
Rubber cement

CONSTRUCTION:
1. Duplicate contraction cards. Cut out and mount on oaktag to make them sturdy.
2. Fold each card along dotted lines as shown. Press along folds with fingernail or spoon to crease well.
3. Open cards and stack them flat.

ACTIVITY:
1. Explain that a contraction is two words shortened into one.
2. Distribute cards and have children examine printed words.
3. Show children how to fold cards to contract words.
4. Ask children to reopen cards and tell which letters have been replaced by an apostrophe. The answer will always be those letters which appear between the two halves of the apostrophe.
5. Make additional contraction cards for those words not covered on the pattern pages. (Note: Some words change their internal spellings to become contractions, such as "won't" from "will not.")

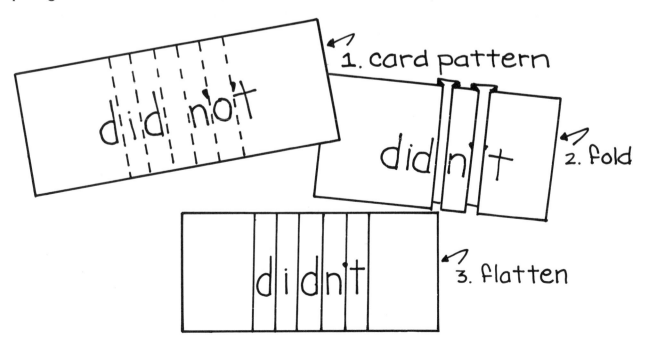

1. card pattern

2. fold

3. flatten

Contraction Cards

did not

I am

we will

what is

Clothesline

Children hang up clothes according to size, kind, color, or number.

OBJECTIVE: To stimulate and encourage classification skills

LEVEL: Preschool - 2

MATERIALS:
Clothes in 3 sizes, different colors
Basket for clothes
Clothesline
Spring-type clothespins stored in plastic bag

CONSTRUCTION:
1. Provide different articles of clothing in different sizes and colors. For example, 3 pairs of pants, 3 T-shirts, 3 socks, 3 sweaters. Store clothes in basket.
2. Place bag of clothespins in clothes basket.
3. Suspend clothesline across part of room or between two chairs. Place basket nearby.

ACTIVITY:
1. Ask children to hang up clothes in size order from smallest to largest for a seriation game.
2. Ask children to hang up all of one kind of clothes for a classification game.
3. Ask children to hang up all the clothes of one color for a color recognition game.
4. Ask children to hang up a specific number of clothing items for a number recognition game.
5. Make clothesline and basket of laundry available so that children can use them as play props to learn on their own.
6. Ask children if they can think of other classifications for sorting clothes, such as dress-up and play clothes, clothes with and without buttons, etc.

Two-Kid Tent

Children can use their imaginations to go on adventures in this classroom play tent.

OBJECTIVE: To encourage dramatic play using props

LEVEL: Preschool - 2

MATERIALS:
Large appliance box (from refrigerator, washer, etc.)
Matte knife
Strapping tape
Camping accessories (optional)

CONSTRUCTION:
1. Cut off top and bottom flaps of appliance box.
2. Cut open along one edge of box.
3. Fold one end of panel over the other to make a triangular shape. Tape panels securely in this position.
4. Set tent in corner of room. Place any camping accessories inside tent.

ACTIVITY:
1. Two children can play in this pup-style tent at one time.
2. Tell students to use their imaginations to make things such as a fire circle out of blocks, a cooking fire with cardboard firewood, or a homemade map for their adventures.
3. Encourage students to act out situations and work out problems creatively and cooperatively.

VARIATION:
• This tent makes a good study prop for social studies units on Gold Rush days, pioneering, and survival training.

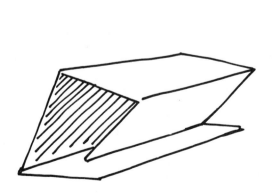

Camping Gear

LANTERN

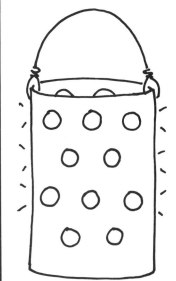

Put small flashlight inside perforated oats carton with lid cut off.

COOKWARE

metal pan, foil-covered ice cream carton, or real soup pot

ladel

WATER BOTTLE

empty plastic milk or juice jug (pint or quart size)

Tie by the handle to belt loop or backpack.

FIREWOOD

cover paper towel rolls with brown paper

blocks for fire circle

cut strips of corrugated cardboard for kindling.

Play Store

Make these display bins for a classroom fruit and vegetable stand, toy store, or snack shop.

OBJECTIVE: To encourage dramatic play

LEVEL: Preschool - 3

MATERIALS:
3 identical rectangular boxes which open on a long panel (such as speaker boxes from a stereo store or envelope cartons from a print shop)
Ruler
Matte knife
White glue
Strapping tape

CONSTRUCTION:
1. Cut off flaps from one box. Find the midpoint of one long edge, then measure three inches in and make a mark, Point A. See diagram.
2. Draw lines from upper left and right corners to Point A. Cut out. Repeat on other side of box.
3. Cut box in half across the base to form two bins.
4. Tape flaps shut on remaining boxes. Turn them on end and glue one bin on top of each. Closed flaps should be on right side of one bin, left side of the other.
5. Position stands side by side to hide the closed flaps between them. Tape together across the back.

ACTIVITY:
1. Stock the play store bins with play foods, toys, or other items.
2. Invite children to go shopping in their classroom store. You may wish to add price tags and play money for a math activity.
3. One tall bin positioned backward can be used as a podium for speaking activities. Positioned forward, it can be a voting booth. A small bin can be used as a doll's highchair. Challenge students to think of more functions for these structures.

Fruit and Vegetable Stand

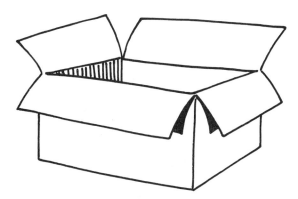

Cut flaps off one box.

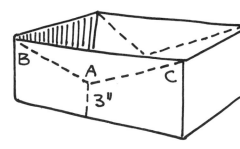

Cut away triangle formed by points A, B, and C on both long sides of box.

Cut apart the bins.

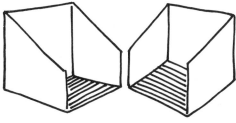

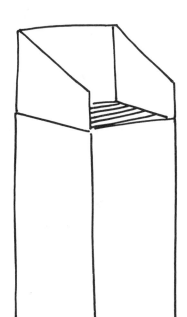

Glue each bin on a box that has been taped together.

Tape together across back.

Restaurant Role Play

Children practice setting and waiting on tables and ordering from menus.

OBJECTIVE: To develop the ability to take orders and make decisions in restaurant situations

LEVEL: Preschool - 3

MATERIALS:
Breakfast, Lunch, and Dinner menus
Fabric remnants for tablecloths
Disposable plates, cups, silverware
Shallow corrugated cardboard box
Pad of paper
Pencil
Food Cutouts
Clear contact paper
Matte knife
Large covered cardboard box

CONSTRUCTION:
1. Duplicate menus and food cutouts. Color, laminate with clear contact paper, and cut out.
2. Cut out two-handled serving tray from corrugated cardboard box.
3. Have children decorate paper plates and cups. (optional)
4. Cut fabric remnant into tablecloths to fit classroom tables.
5. Store all materials in large cardboard box when not in use.

ACTIVITY:
1. Select children to be waiters, waitresses, and customers.
2. Have waiters and waitresses set the tables, give menus to customers, and take their orders.
3. Waiters and waitresses serve the orders, using tray and food cutouts.
4. Encourage children to be clear and exact in giving and taking orders. Help them use appropriate language in this social interaction.

VARIATION:
● For older students, add prices to the menus. Have waiters and waitresses add up bills and make change from play money.

Menus

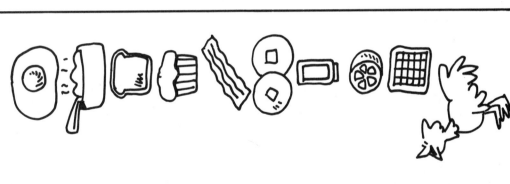

LUNCH MENU

Sandwich
Soup
Hot Dog
Hamburger
Beans
Carrot
Apple
Grapes
Cookie

BREAKFAST MENU

Egg
Cereal
Toast
Muffin
Bacon
Pancakes
Milk
Orange
Waffle

Menu and Food Cutouts

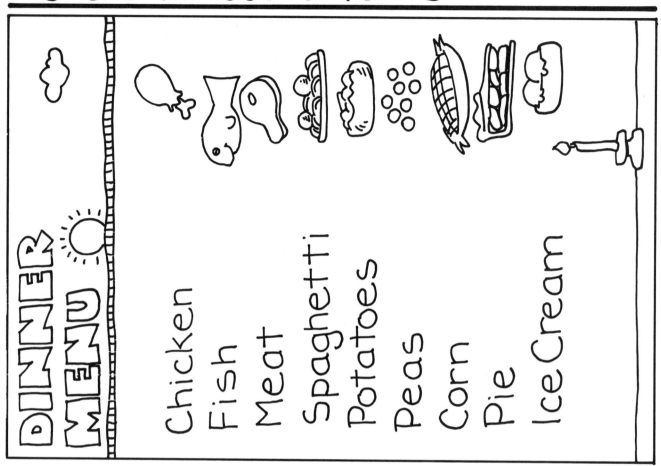

DINNER MENU

Chicken
Fish
Meat
Spaghetti
Potatoes
Peas
Corn
Pie
Ice Cream

Food Cutouts

Food Cutouts

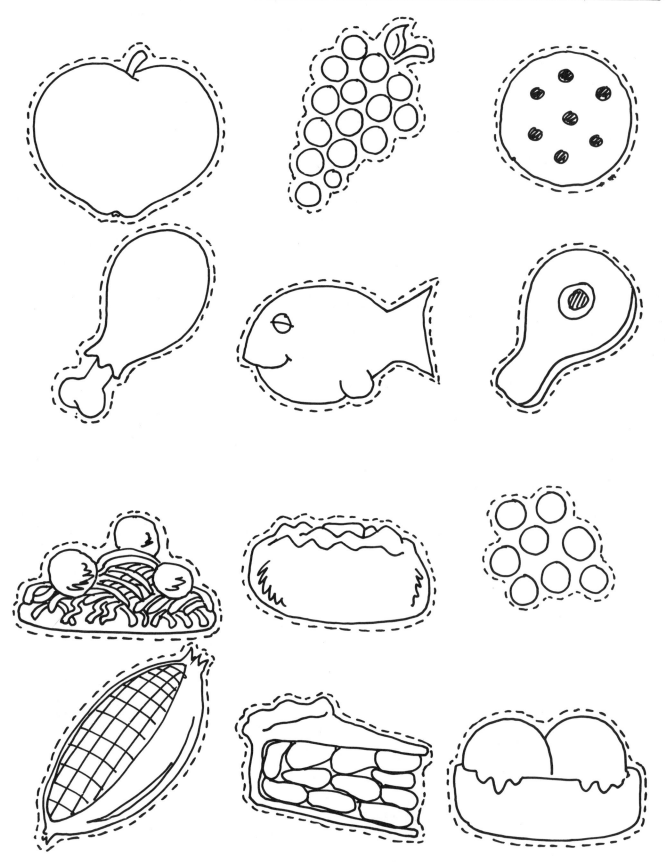

Classroom Management

All Aboard

A train conductor collects children's tickets every day on this attendance bulletin board.

OBJECTIVE: To facilitate taking attendance

LEVEL: K - 3

MATERIALS:
Train, Conductor, Ticket patterns
Opaque projector
Colored construction paper
Library pockets (one per child)
Marker Photos of students (optional)
Glue Empty tissue or shoe box

CONSTRUCTION:
1. Tape 2 large pieces of construction paper to bare wall and project train and conductor patterns at 300%. Trace and cut out.
2. Duplicate train tickets, on colored paper if possible. Cut apart to make one for each child.
3. Print each child's name on a library pocket. If you like, paste on child's photo as well.
4. Staple colored paper backing to bulletin board. Staple train with caption to the top of the board, conductor in lower right corner, and library pockets in rows to his left.
5. Staple box to bulletin board between conductor's hands. Fold up hands and paste to sides of box.
6. Place a ticket in each pocket.

ACTIVITY:
1. Children remove their tickets from the pockets upon entering the classroom and deposit them in the conductor's box.
2. Teacher notes absentees by checking for uncollected tickets.
3. Select an assistant conductor each day to replace the tickets for the next day's attendance.

Train and Conductor

Train Tickets

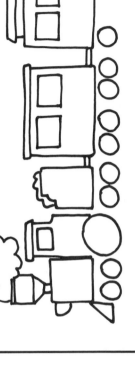

TRAIN TICKET

Give this ticket to the conductor and climb aboad!

TRAIN TICKET

Give this ticket to the conductor and climb aboad!

TRAIN TICKET

Give this ticket to the conductor and climb aboad!

TRAIN TICKET

Give this ticket to the conductor and climb aboad!

Bookworm Apples

To chart their reading progress, your bookworms can take a bite of their apples every time they finish a qualifying activity.

OBJECTIVE: To motivate students to finish assignments

LEVEL: 2 and up

MATERIALS:
Apple, Bookworm patterns
Red poster board
Black marker
Hole punch
Thumbtacks

CONSTRUCTION:
1. Trace apple for each student on red poster board.
2. Duplicate apple core block for each student. After children have filled in their names, mount blocks on bulletin board.
3. Tack an apple over each core, lining up stems.

ACTIVITY:
1. After completing a book, story, report, or other reading assignment, student can remove apple and punch a prescribed number of holes anywhere along outside edge.
2. Student replaces apple on core until more bites are earned. Holes must be punched from outside in and must touch edge of previous bite. Object is to eat away at apple to reveal entire core.
3. While each child munches on an individual apple, the whole class, or whole school, can work together on one giant apple. This is an excellent way to foster group spirit and teamwork.

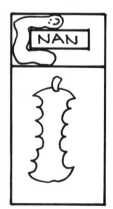 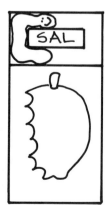 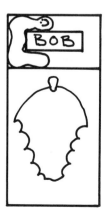 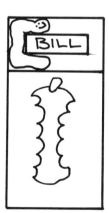  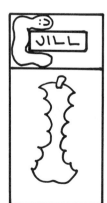

Bookworm Apples

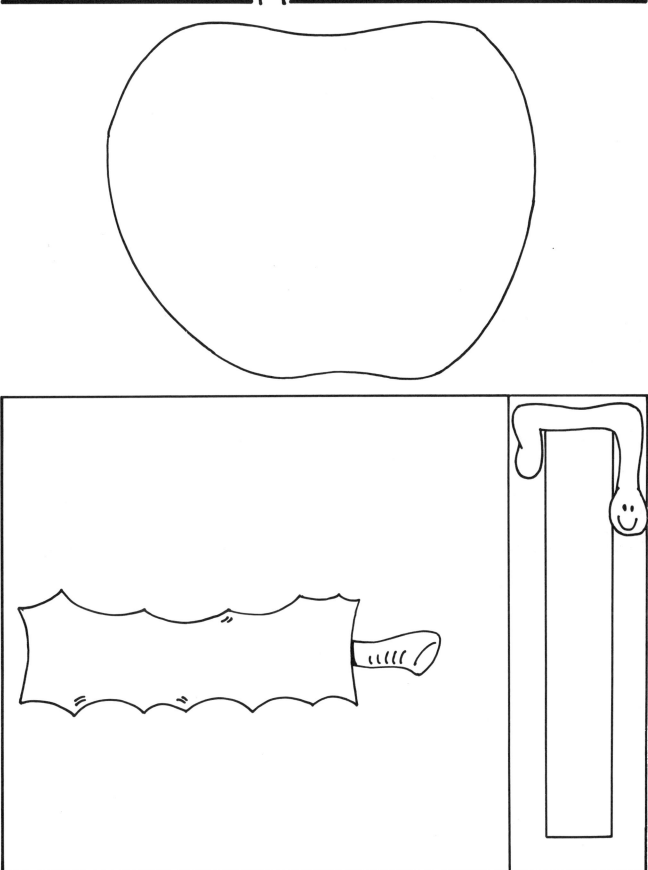

Parking Lot Attendance

A parking lot attendant takes attendance in this three-dimensional roll call.

MATERIALS:
Large shallow box
Matte knife or knife with serrated edge
Large sheet of white paper
Clear contact paper
Grease pencil or erasable crayon
White glue or rubber cement
Small toy cars
Shoebox or other container for cars

CONSTRUCTION:
1. Cut off one panel of box as shown.
2. Cut paper to fit bottom of box.
3. Draw parking spaces on paper to correspond to seating arrangement in classroom. Be sure parking spaces are large enough to fit cars.
4. Decorate interior of parking lot. Then glue paper to bottom of box and cover with clear contact paper. Write names of students in parking spaces with grease pencil or erasable crayon. If seating changes, you can easily remove and rewrite names.
5. Let each child choose a car and write his or her name on it.
6. Store cars in shoebox, which you may wish to decorate.

ACTIVITY:
1. When students arrive in the morning, have them place their cars in the proper parking spaces.
2. Have students take turns being parking lot attendant. Attendant checks to see who is absent and reports this information to the teacher.
3. You may wish to call the names of the absentees as a further check.

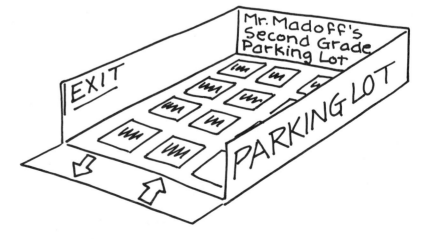

Trading Stamps

Children can earn trading stamps worth special privileges for completed tasks or assignments.

OBJECTIVE: To motivate students to complete assignments

LEVEL: 2 and up

MATERIALS:
Trading Stamp Book pattern
Peel-off labels in several colors for trading stamps
Report folder

CONSTRUCTION:
1. Duplicate stamp book pattern page.
2. Cut out books on solid lines, fold on dotted lines. (Children can cut and fold their own books.)
3. Use report folder to make a "premium catalog." Label the folder. On first page list assignments that qualify for a trading stamp. (Some work may be worth more than one stamp.) Add to list as you make new assignments. On following pages list special privileges or prizes that can be redeemed for a complete book of stamps. Suggestions: free period, stickers, novelty eraser, comic book, new pencil.

ACTIVITY:
1. Give children stamps whenever they fulfill a required assignment.
2. When a child fills a book, the child can redeem the book for any item listed in catalog.
3. Child receives another stamp book to continue the collection.

fold in half...

and half again

Trading Stamp Book

2

1

1ST
FOLD

Date Completed: _____

   This book is redeemable for one gift from the trading stamp catalog. Write the gift you would like on the line below:

_____

Collect Valuable

TRADING STAMPS

ONE BOOK

NAME _____

2ND FOLD

Punching In

Punch cards reinforce the sense of accomplishment for completed homework or daily attendance.

OBJECTIVE: To encourage homework completion or daily attendance

LEVEL: 3 and up

MATERIALS:
Punch Cards
Punch-In Sheet
Clear contact paper
Hole punch

CONSTRUCTION:
1. List the names of students by rows on Punch-In Sheet. Duplicate this page for each day of the marking period.
2. Duplicate punch card page to provide one card per child per month. Laminate cards with clear contact paper before cutting them apart. (To make cards sturdier without laminating, have them printed on cardstock at a copy shop.)

ACTIVITY:
1. Give each child a punch card. Have children write in their names. (If cards are laminated, they will need to use crayons.)
2. Assign a different child each week the job of taking attendance or collecting homework. At the start of the day, this child punches each student's card for attendance or for completed homework, then punches the block next to each student's name on the Punch-In Sheet.
3. Student helper returns cards to classmates and gives Punch-In Sheet to teacher, who can quickly spot absentees or those who did not do homework.

Punch Cards

PUNCH·CARD

NAME _____

DATE _____

PUNCH·CARD

NAME _____

DATE _____

PUNCH·CARD

NAME _____

DATE _____

PUNCH·CARD

NAME _____

DATE _____

Punch In

	DATE: ___ NAMES		
◯			◯

Job Board

Classroom job descriptions are posted on this bulletin board. Students must assess their own personal skills.

OBJECTIVES: To learn to assess personal skills and apply for jobs

LEVEL: 3 and up

MATERIALS:
Job Application
Construction paper for bulletin board backing
Plain paper for job listings
Felt-tip pen
File folder for each job listing
Cardboard box in which file folders stand upright
Empty tissue box

CONSTRUCTION:
1. On each piece of paper list a different classroom job, its description, and a few skills or attributes the ideal candidate for the job would have. Store each job listing in a separate file folder, with the job title printed on the tab at the top.
2. Staple backing to bulletin board. Use a second color for the door on one side of the board.
3. Staple sign on door that reads Employment Office. To the right, at top of bulletin board, staple letters for Job Board.
4. Label front of box Job Files. Tack back of box to lower right corner of bulletin board. Place folders inside box.
5. Cut away top of tissue box. Label one long side panel Applications. Tack tissue box to bulletin board near files.
6. Duplicate job application so that each child has at least one. Letter-fold applications and place them in the applications box.

ACTIVITY:
1. Help children read job descriptions and encourage them to talk about their special interests and abilities.
2. Invite children to fill out job applications and place them in the appropriate job file. Explain that you will read the applications and "hire" one or more children for each job.
3. You can hire both full-time employees to hold jobs for the whole school year, and part-time workers to take turns. Applications ask for second choice jobs, so no one should be sorely disappointed.
4. Post a list of full-time and part-time workers on the bulletin board for reference.

WASHING THE BLACKBOARD

I need two children to take turns staying an extra 5 minutes at the end of the day to wash the board.

Children must be tall, steady on a chair, and reliable. Only children who walk or ride bikes to school should apply. Those who take the bus must leave too early.

Job Board

Job Application

JOB APPLICATION
_____

Your Name _____

Job Title: _____

Please write a sentence telling why you
would like this job.

_____

_____

Please list two or three things about yourself
that make you a good person for this job.

1. _____

_____

2. _____

_____

3. _____

_____

List another job you read about on
the job board that you might enjoy.

_____